The Backstreet Boys

Maggie Marron

BARNES & NOBLE BOOKS
NEW YORK

Dedication
To Backstreet Bob M.

This edition published by Barnes & Noble, Inc.
by arrangement with Michael Friedman
Publishing Group, Inc.

2000 Barnes & Noble Books

© 2000 by Michael Friedman Publishing
Group, Inc.

ISBN 0-7607-2001-0

1 3 5 7 9 10 8 6 4 2

Editor: Ann Kirby
Art Director: Kevin Ullrich
Designer: Liz Travato
Photography Editor: Valerie E. Kennedy
Production Manager: Richela Fabian

Printed in England by Butler & Tanner Ltd.
Color separations by Radstock Repro

The Boys, just before they
took off for Europe.
Clockwise from top: A.J.
McLean, Brian Littrell, Nick
Carter, Kevin Richardson,
and Howie Dorough.

Contents

Introduction

"We hope to be old people onstage together, as old as the Rolling Stones."

—Nick, in *USA Weekend,*
January 1999

The guys look tough
filming a commercial for
Sears, the sponsor of
their 1999 tour.

It seems like these days you can't turn on the radio or television or open a magazine without getting a glimpse of the Backstreet Boys—the five gorgeous hunks based in Orlando, Florida, who have captured the hearts of millions of women around the world with their excellent tunes and killer dance moves.

Sure, today the group might be a household name, but an overnight success the guys have not been—at least not in their native country. As a matter of fact, just a couple of years ago they could all be walking down a street in the States and no one would give them the time of day—let alone clamor for an autograph or a lock of hair. Now, all that's changed.

It took years of struggling—singing and dancing their hearts out, trotting across the globe, making records, getting signed, getting dropped, hiring managers, firing managers—and, for many of the guys, overcoming personal strife to get where they are today. And what if they had given up? Where would we be today without Nick's impish smile, or A.J.'s crazy tattoos, or Kevin's dreamy eyes, or Howie's impeccable sweetness, or Brian's velvety smooth voice? We'd be totally deprived of the experience of a lifetime— that's where we'd be!

The Backstreet Boys have made their way into our hearts for more than just their music. Each member is as interesting as the next and each is unique. And they're all very talented. "You usually don't get five people who can sing *a cappella* like they can, minus the engineers and producers," Hedy End, editorial director of *SuperTeen* and *Superstars* magazines, has said. Plus, these guys don't just sing; they dance, they write some of their own music, and most of them play musical instruments. And to top it all off— they're all cute!

The Backstreet Boys are everyone's favorite boys next door, and the guys who started it all—the ones who opened the door for acts like 'N Sync, 98°, and 5ive, and set a new standard in the contemporary music world. And the best thing about the guys is that they love their fans, probably even more than their fans love them! As they sing in their song "Larger Than Life" (a tribute to their fans): "All of your time spent keeps us alive . . ."

Now turn the page and learn the story of the sexiest guy group around!

Black leather jackets, black jeans, and black boots—
Backstreet Boys are stylin' on stage.

Chapter One
Beginnings

"Yeah, people will look at us and see an automatic stereotype. But once they hear us, they'll know we're for real."

—Howie, in *Entertainment Weekly*, August 1997

The guys in London. The Backstreet Boys made a huge splash in London, while in their own country they were virtual unknowns.

There's more than one version out there of the story of how the Backstreet Boys got started. One story says that the group was the brainchild of talent manager Louis Pearlman, the "father" of such acts as 'N Sync. Another says that the guys were handpicked and assembled by the talent management firm The Wright Stuff. And yet another says that each of the guys was looking to fulfill the dream of becoming a world-class performer, and eventually they found each other. In a sense, all three stories are true.

Each member of the Backstreet Boys has a unique look, style, and talent, yet the quintet works incredibly well together. That's part of the group's appeal.

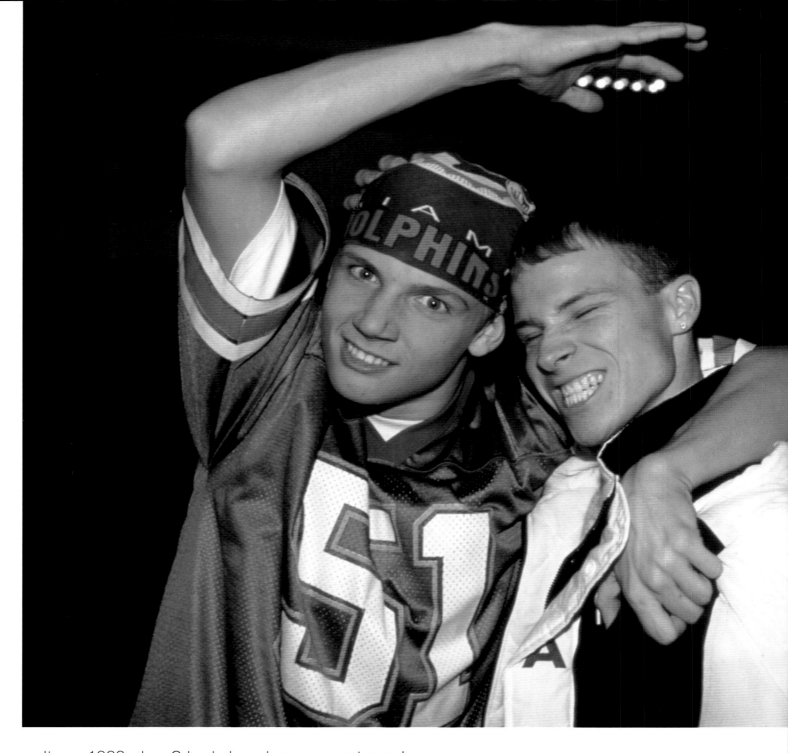

It was 1993 when Orlando-based management guru Lou Pearlman decided that the time was right once again to introduce a new guy group onto the music scene. There wasn't a group out there at that moment that tugged at the heartstrings and infiltrated the daydreams of young girls everywhere. By that time, the New Kids were "out"—way out. Instead, girls had to content themselves with messy grunge rockers like Nirvana's Kurt Cobain and Pearl Jam's Eddie Vedder. Pearlman brought in Johnny and Donna Wright, the masterminds behind the New Kids on the Block phenomenon, to get the project rolling. The Wrights quickly placed an ad in a national newspaper looking for talent to create a band in the vein of their last success story.

Nick and Brian mug for the cameras. All the Boys are as close as brothers.

What Makes the Backstreet Boys Stand Out?

The Backstreet Boys have certainly spawned their fair share of copycat acts, even one created by Lou Pearlman himself—we'll get to that in a minute! But what makes the Backstreet Boys a one-of-a-kind group? That's pretty easy to answer.

There are of course the obvious reasons. There's someone for everyone to love in the group. They're all different ages and each has his own look and distinct personality. And they can all sing—and how! On top of that, Howie and Brian both play the guitar, Nick is teaching himself the drums, and Kevin's been playing the piano by ear since he could walk—plus they all like to write their own songs.

At the heart of it, what really makes them strong is their dedication to each other. The Boys are like brothers, and it is this special bond that will keep them together for the long haul, while they develop their talents as a group. They've already been together for more than five years and have been through lots of struggles in that time and managed to stay together—what could possibly come between them now? As Nick told *Teen* magazine in September of 1998, "Several groups have let fans down by breaking up. We've been together for five years. We're gonna stick around." And A.J. continued, "Since the group started, it's always been five, and I don't think anybody's going anywhere fast. It will always be the five of us—[we're] like brothers."

"We're thankful we came first, but everybody that came behind us . . . we did a lot of opening doors [for them]," Brian confidently told *Teen People*. "I think we'll continue to do that." Of course Howie, Mr. Diplomacy, also acknowledged that "There were a lot of people who opened the doors for us before in the past. It's always just a process of helping each other out and stuff. Like I say, I don't look at it as a competition thing—if anything, it's a friendly competition."

Part of the supposed "rivalry" that the media likes to set up between 'N Sync and the Backstreet Boys is that they have the same "father," namely Lou Pearlman, though the Backstreet Boys came first. "That hurt our feelings," Kevin confided to *Rolling Stone*. "Because it was like, 'We're a family.' Then all of a sudden, 'It's business guys, sorry.' We have nothing against . . . that group personally. It was Pearlman not being honest."

The guys of 'N Sync have nothing against the Boys either. "Honestly," JC Chasez, the leader of the group told the *Los Angeles Times*, "they're busy doing their thing and we're busy doing ours."

Who has more staying power? Only time will tell, but it's nice to know that at the bottom of it all the guys in both groups might actually really be friends!

Backstreet Quiz How well do you know **The Early Days**

1) Before joining the Backstreet Boys, Kevin was working as:
a. Clown
b. Aladdin at Disney World
c. Waiter
d. Ice-cream man

2) Who was the last Boy to sign up?
a. Howie
b. Nick
c. Brian
d. A.J.

3) Which Boy has other famous family members?
a. Nick
b. Kevin
c. A.J.
d. Howie

4) Which guy's mother wrote a best-selling book about his early days?
a. A.J.
b. Howie
c. Nick
d. Kevin

5) Which Boy has always read the Bible to wind down from a crazy day?
a. Brian
b. Howie
c. Nick
d. A.J.

Answers: 1: b; 2: c; 3: a; 4: c; 5: a

In the meantime, the everyday, ordinary guys that would become the international superstars they are today were leading pretty everyday, ordinary lives. Florida natives Howie Dorough and A.J. McLean, who today are best buds, had gotten acquainted on the Florida talent circuit, often bumping into each other at the same auditions. The two of them began to pal around together at the auditions, until they started to notice another kid—a blond-haired, blue-eyed crooner who could sing like nobody's business. And then there were three.

Nick Carter, Howie, and A.J. became very serious about performing with each other and even got a group together and performed as an *a cappella* act. They called themselves "The Backstreet Boys" after a market in Orlando where kids hang out. One day, while shuffling through the entertainment-jobs section of the paper, they came across the Wrights' ad. Convinced that this was the right way for them to go, the guys answered the ad and promptly auditioned. They almost all didn't make it in, however—but not for lack of talent. Howie had changed his name for the audition to "Tony Donetti," and in the shuffle of all the guys who came through the door for the audition, his "name" was misplaced. It's a good thing his pals Nick and A.J. landed their spots. They were able to clear up the confusion; the slots were then more than half filled.

Elsewhere in Florida, Kentuckian Kevin Richardson was working as Aladdin in the Disney World theme park when he came across the same ad. Although he was enjoying his stint as the famous Disney character by day, and spinning discs and clubbing by night, he knew somehow that this sounded like what he had been looking for all along. Kevin auditioned and became the fourth Backstreet Boy. It was a nightmare, though, trying to fit in the last piece. "I saw two people, and it was pretty bad," Kevin told *Rolling Stone*. "It just made me sad. And I said, 'You know what? I have a cousin who can sing his butt off.'" Brian Littrell auditioned, and the Backstreet Boys as we know them today were born.

The next step was to get this baby group the attention it deserved—and, of course, a record label to sign them. There was no doubt about the group's talent. Donna Wright told the *Los Angeles Times*, "My whole career, I've always gone with instinct. When I first heard the Backstreet Boys, I got the chills so strong that the hairs stood up straight on the back of my neck. I could just tell there was something there." Now it was just a matter of convincing the rest of the world.

Opposite: An early shot of A.J.—pre–tattoos, wacky hair, and crazy get-ups.

The team decided that the best way to get the guys noticed was to start making fans first. That way, they could prove to record company executives that even though there weren't yet any groups out there like the Backstreet Boys, there was definitely an audience for them. The truth is that they knew that once the guys proved themselves, it wouldn't be a matter of convincing a record label to sign them—the record labels would be fighting each other to the death in order to be the lucky one that signed the group. So the guys began a grueling tour of the States, performing at high schools, parties, whatever it took to get noticed. They were signed up by S.A.D.D. (Students Against Drunk Driving) to become ambassadors, giving them a higher profile. But it still wasn't enough.

Mercury Records initially picked up the guys in 1994, but they were almost immediately dropped when the label decided they weren't interested in the "guy group" thing. Records by Snoop Doggie Dogg and Aerosmith were flying off the shelves at record stores. How could five clean-cut boys singing angelic harmonies *a cappella* compete?

Pearlman couldn't give the Backstreet Boys away. At that point the labels had other plans. "It was hard. Lou shopped the group to ten different labels and nobody was interested. Everybody said the so-called boy band thing is over. Nobody knew these guys or wanted to," Alan Siegel, a longtime associate of Pearlman, told the *Los Angeles Times*. But Pearlman wouldn't give up. He fought to get the Boys a deal, and they were finally signed to Jive Records, a fairly new label under the Bertelsmann Music Group umbrella, in 1994. There was a lot of excitement when the Boys released their very first single, "We've Got It Goin' On," in October of 1995.

No one involved, from the guys to the Wrights to Lou Pearlman to the executives at Jive, thought they could lose. But they were wrong. The song peaked at an obscure number sixty-nine on the charts. The world at large still didn't know about the Backstreet Boys.

Kevin performs one of his solos in concert.

Luckily, the team was savvy enough to release the single in Europe as well. "We were right. They exploded," Johnny Wright explained to the *Los Angeles Times*. What had seemed like a reason to throw in the towel in the States soon became a sensation across the Atlantic. "We've Got It Goin' On" was huge overseas, especially in Germany, where it almost immediately hit number one. At that point, everyone knew what had to be done. The Backstreet Boys would start out in Europe, and, they hoped, eventually American audiences would begin to catch on.

These pages: Kevin, the leader and dreamboat, and A.J.

Nick Carter

"I consider myself 'a modern-day hermit' . . . I like to just sit around in my house and hide away."

—Nick, in *SuperTeen*, August 1999

Nick, decked out in full Miami Dolphins fan-wear.

The youngest of the Backstreet Boys, Nick Carter definitely plays the little brother role well, mostly by playing practical jokes on his older brothers. But the guys get along great when all is said and done, and Nick loves his bandmates as if they really were his brothers. In fact, he counts Brian Littrell as his very best friend.

"I think in order to stay together for a long time you have to have communication," he has said. "You have to be able to talk with each other. And I think we established that pretty much a long time ago. We treat this basically like a family of five brothers, you know. And we just make sure that anything that pops up, we, you know, nail it right in the butt." Nip it in the bud, nail it in the butt—whatever. The important thing is that they all try hard to keep it together.

Stand back ladies—in crooner mode, Nick is a real heartbreaker.

"The Cute One": Nick's Vital Stats

Full name: **Nicholas Gene Carter**

Millennium element: **Water**

Birth date: **January 28, 1980**

Star sign: **Aquarius**

Hair: **Blond**

Eyes: **Gray-Blue**

Height: **6'1"**

Parents' names: **Jane and Bob Carter**

Brothers and sisters: **Bobbie Jean (BJ), Leslie, and the twins, Aaron and Angel**

Pets: **Boo Boo (a terrier) and Pinky (a cat)**

Nicknames: **Nick, Nicky, Chaos**

Hobbies: **Water sports**

Special trait: **Nick is the joker of the group, which is why the guys call him Chaos.**

Special skill: **Nick is a certified scuba diver.**

Perfect mate: **She has to like aquatic activities to keep up with Nick's passion for the beach—and, oh yeah, it wouldn't hurt if she knew her way around an arcade!**

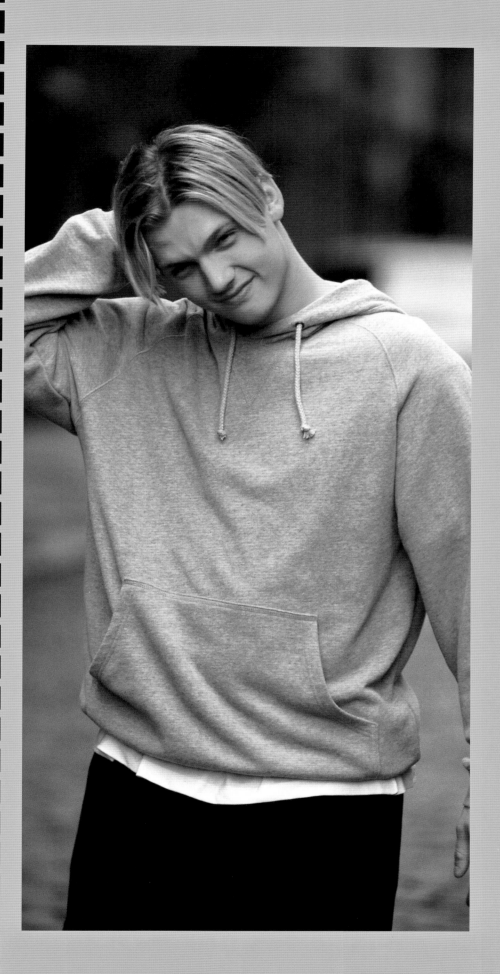

Nick looks amazing even in a hooded sweatshirt!

Above: Nick at the *Millennium* press conference—a tangerine dream!

Opposite: Nick belts out a solo during the 1997 U.S. tour.

Nicholas Gene Carter was born in Jamestown, New York, in the same hospital as the legendary comedienne Lucille Ball. Did that have anything to do with his eventual fame? Maybe a teeny tiny bit, but Nick is all talent, which his family acknowledged at a very early age (it had to have been early—Nick was only thirteen when he signed up with BSB!). When Nick was six, his parents moved the family—Nick and his baby sister BJ—to Tampa Bay, Florida.

Nick's first crack at show business was a leading role in a school production of *The Phantom of the Opera*. (No, he didn't play the phantom! He played the romantic lead, Raoul.) His performance got raves and prompted him to start a career in acting. At nine years old, he began doing commercials—both local and national—and then decided what he really loved more than anything was singing.

In the early 1990s, Nick auditioned for *The Mickey Mouse Club*, the same show that would launch the careers of Britney Spears, Keri Russell, and 'N Sync members Justin Timberlake and JC Chasez. But another opportunity was looming not too far off in the distance. By this point, Nick had already befriended Howie Dorough and A.J. McClean, and the three had formed a singing group together. When the offers to become a Mouseketeer or a Backstreet Boy came through at nearly the same time, Nick had a hard decision on his hands. *The Mickey Mouse Club* was already well established; the Backstreet Boys would be the riskier choice. But Nick decided to take that chance, which was the best career move he could have made—*The Mickey Mouse Club* was canceled shortly after Nick was offered a part.

Above: Nick poses with his mom, Jane, at a signing for her book, *The Heart and Soul of Nick Carter*.

Opposite: Nick showing off his dance moves onstage.

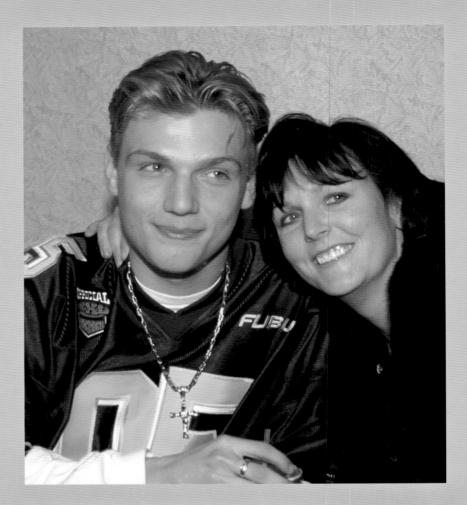

The World Famous Carter Brothers!

The Carter family sure has a lot to brag about these days! Not only is their oldest boy, Nick, a superstar with the Backstreet Boys, but Nick's brother, Aaron, has also caused a sensation in his own right. Just eleven years old, Aaron—whose favorite thing about being a pop star is that "fans give me candy all the time!"—has become a name well known and revered not only in his own country but all over Europe, in Asia, and in Canada as well.

So is there any rivalry between the two brothers? Not any more than there would be between any other pair of siblings. But the pair benefits from a lot of support and encouragement for each another. For example, Aaron was the opening act on the Backstreet Boys 1998 tour. Also, Nick, with the help of BSB "brother" Brian Littrell, wrote a couple of the songs on Aaron's album, *Surfin' USA*, including, "Ain't That Cute." As for Aaron's part, he's looking forward to his big brother making lots of appearances on his new TV show, which is in the negotiations stage at this writing.

Lucky Nick: Not many guys are fortunate to have so many great brothers!

BACKSTREET QUIZ How well do you know . . . Nick?

1. Nick's favorite cereal is:
a. Alpha Bits
b. Froot Loops
c. Count Chocula
d. Frosted Flakes

2. When's he's not jamming with the guys, Nick's favorite music to listen to is:
a. Rap
b. Pop
c. Jazz
d. Classical

3. Nick's favorite movie is:
a. *I Know What You Did Last Summer*
b. *Aliens*
c. *She's All That*
d. *Scream*

4. Nick doesn't watch a lot of TV (he's too busy playing video games!), but when he does, he never misses:
a. *Seinfeld*
b. *ER*
c. *Felicity*
d. *Mad About You*

5. Nick's favorite actress is:
a. Alicia Silverstone
b. Sigourney Weaver
c. Pamela Anderson
d. Keri Russell

Answers: 1: c; 2: a; 3: b; 4: d; 5: b

In many ways, Nick has gotten most of the attention from fans. His blond locks and drop-dead gray-blue eyes are too irresistible for most women to ignore! As much as Nick likes the attention from his fans, however, he sometimes feels that they're not appreciating him for the right things. "Screaming is all right," he said in *USA Weekend*. "But if you want to approach us, come say, 'Hi, we respect your music.' That's what we're all about: music." And, besides, his fans are more concerned with his looks than he is—he couldn't care less what he walks around in, which are usually baggy jeans and an equally baggy shirt. And why does he wear hats so often? Well, it's not for vanity, that's for sure. "I don't care if people see me with my hair sticking out there," he told *Teen People*. "It's just me."

Opposite: People say that Nick looks like Leonardo DiCaprio. . . . Nah! Nick is much cuter!

Chapter Three
Brian Littrell

"I think everyone is here for a reason. I think it's destiny that we're all together."

—Brian, in *Backstreet Boys Confidential: The Unofficial Book*

Brian and friend mug for the cameras.

"The Shy One": Brian's Vital Stats

Full name: **Brian Thomas Littrell**

Millennium element: **Air**

Birth date: **February 20, 1975**

Star sign: **Pisces**

Hair: **Brown**

Eyes: **Blue**

Height: **5' 8"**

Parents' names: **Jackie and Harold Littrell, Jr.**

Brother: **Harold Littrell III**

Pets: **Lil' Tyke (a Chihuahua)**

Nickname: **B-Rok**

Hobbies: **Playing basketball, lifting weights, listening to music**

Special trait: **Brian is the most religious of the guys and goes to church just about every Sunday.**

Special skill: **Brian's really good at basketball, which is why the guys call him B-Rok, and might have tried to go pro if the Backstreet Boys had never happened.**

Perfect mate: **Brian has a girlfriend now, which is nice because he's always happiest when he's involved in a steady relationship.**

BRIAN

Above: Daydreaming about the upcoming *Millennium* tour during a group press conference.

Opposite: Brian and his blond-haired girlfriend (she's right behind him) sneak into New York hot spot Mars for the *Phantom Menace* premiere party.

Nineteeen Ninety-Eight was our most successful year," Brian Littrell told *Rolling Stone*. "It was also the hardest year of my life." Without a doubt, Brian is the guy that has had the biggest personal obstacle to overcome for his fame. You see, Brian was born with a heart murmur that wasn't discovered until he was five years old, when his heart actually stopped! Brian had to stay in the hospital for two months, an experience he still has nightmares about. He seemed to be doing fine after that—up until he started touring heavily with the Boys and working all the time. Then, his health took a change for the worse.

"After six years of a schedule that was pretty much horrendous, he went for his annual checkup and the doctors noticed that his heart was getting quite large, like one for a 300-pound linebacker," Brian's mom, Jackie, said in *Rolling Stone*. There was no choice. Brian needed surgery—and fast. He put the surgery off to fulfill some commitments with the band, but soon enough he found he couldn't hold out anymore. It was less than two months after his open-heart surgery that he joined the guys on the road again. Would he put something so serious like that off again for work? Not a chance. The experience taught Brian what his priorities are. "Music is my love," he told *Rolling Stone*, "but it's my job. There are things that used to be taken for granted that aren't now: time with your family, time to enjoy the fruits of your labor."

Brian grew up in Lexington, Kentucky, where his family was very active in the church. His mother sang at services, which is how Brian got his start singing. When he was six, he sang his first solo in front of the congregation and brought down the house. He continued to pursue singing and performing, but more so as a hobby than a serious vocation. In fact, he was on his way to college at the University of Cincinnati Bible College on a scholarship for singing when he got the news that he had made it into the Backstreet Boys.

These pages: Some early shots of Brian, "the shy one." The crucifix he wears around his neck is more than a fashion statement— Brian is a devout Christian.

Brian is known as "the shy one," and this could not be more true. It even comes out in his performance style. For instance, during the show he likes singing his solo while sitting in a chair, strumming his guitar. "It's a very personal experience and that's what I wanted it to be," he told *Teen Beat.* "Sitting down—if they didn't want to scream than they didn't have to, they could just sit and listen and watch. That was my whole idea because the show

Brian acts as ball boy for Arthur Ashe Tennis Day.

Brian relaxes during a photo shoot for Sears. The company is sponsoring the BSB '99 tour.

Backstreet Quiz How well do you know...**Brian?**

1) Brian's favorite movie is:
a. *You've Got Mail*
b. *Scream*
c. *Star Wars*
d. *The Breakfast Club*

2) What's Brian's favorite food?
a. Fried chicken
b. Macaroni and cheese
c. Steak
d. Tacos

3) Brian's favorite color is:
a. Midnight blue
b. Burnt orange
c. Forest green
d. Bright red

4) Brian is most afraid of:
a. Spiders
b. Heights
c. Snakes
d. Enclosed spaces

5) Brian's favorite movie actress is:
a. Julia Roberts
b. Elizabeth Hurley
c. Meg Ryan
d. Sandra Bullock

Answers: 1: c; 2: b; 3: a; 4: b; 5: d

is so bing, bang, boom, and then we have the five solos, and even those are bing, bang, boom, and I'm not really like that . . . when it can be really personal, I just walk out, show people who I am."

Brian certainly likes the attention of his fans but, like Nick, as well as the other guys, he wants to be appreciated for his talent, not just his sex appeal. Sometimes he doesn't even understand why girls get themselves so worked up when they see him. He told *Rolling Stone* that when they approach him, "[I] say, 'I'm human, it's no big deal.'"

Brian pals around with all the guys, but Nick Carter is definitely his best friend—despite their age difference and the way Nick has picked on his accent: "When I first met [Brian], I thought, COUNTRY BUMPKIN! It was crazy! 'Heyyy, howww ya'lll dooooin'? My name's Briaaaaan Littrell,'" Nick laughed, in *SuperTeen*. When Howie, Kevin, and A.J. hit the club scene, Brian stays in with Nick—who's under twenty-one—and the two play video games. They have become such great friends, in fact, that they are known in the band—and to their fans—as Frick and Frack.

Chapter Four

Around the World...in 730 Days

"[International] success has made us more well rounded. It changed our perspectives on the way the world is."

—Kevin, in *Billboard* magazine, November 1997

The Boys on stage. Touring is fun, but it's also hard work.

When the guys couldn't even hail a cab in the States in 1995, they headed across the pond to try their luck in foreign markets. What an experience it proved to be for them. Such excitement! Such hysteria! The world hadn't seen anything like it since the Beatles touched down on American soil more than thirty years earlier.

For the next two years, the Backstreet Boys would tour almost nonstop (how about five tours in one year!), which put a toll on their lives in more ways than one. Although the stardom was exhilarating, the guys really missed home.

All the Boys are very close to their families and no attention from their fans could replace the void they often felt on the road. "We like our families to be able to turn on the TV and see what we're doing," Kevin told *People Weekly*. Still, it wasn't the same as being home with them. They missed ". . . our families, our home-cooked meals, our own beds," Howie has admitted. A.J. agrees and is sad that fame "really limited our time with our friends and families," but added that "You can kind of get better Christmas presents for your family and stuff like that."

BACKSTREET QUIZ How well do you know . . . The Backstreet Tour Experience?

1) Which Boys love to dine in different countries, getting a sample of that country's cuisine?
a. Howie and A.J.
b. Nick and Brian
c. Kevin and A.J.
d. Kevin and Howie

2) Which of the Boys toured South America—without the others?
a. Howie
b. Kevin
c. A.J.
d. Nick

3) Where did "We've Got It Goin' On" first hit number one?
a. Sweden
b. Germany
c. France
d. Canada

4) Which Boy refuses to eat dairy products before a performance because he fears they cloud his voice?
a. Nick
b. A.J.
c. Brian
d. Kevin

5) Who takes the longest to get ready for a show?
a. Brian
b. Kevin
c. A.J.
d. Nick

Brian, A.J., Nick (sticking his tongue out), and Howie—is Kevin taking the picture?

Answers: 1: d; 2: a; 3: b; 4: d; 5: c

Being away from their families is not something the guys really want to get used to. And then there was Brian's heart problem . . .

The Boys got their first taste of superstardom in Germany, where their single "We've Got It Goin' On" reached number one almost as soon as it hit the airwaves. The Boys will all tell you that their experiences in Europe were a trip and a half! The fans were, well, fanatical, and they would show up in the oddest places just to get close to the guys. Brian remembered for *USA Today* that, one day, "I drove into my apartment complex, and they know my car because a picture of it had been in a magazine. And these two girls—one was from Germany and one was from Switzerland—were sitting right in front of my apartment with their pens and paper, and they jumped as soon as they saw me."

Howie agrees that their European fans were definitely aggressive. "We used to talk to fans in the hotel lobby, but we can't be as personable with our European fans because the hype is so big over there," he said in *Teen* magazine. Nick confirmed, in

USA Today, that "We've been on radio stations in Germany and had to climb out of the windows to get out of the place. But in the end, it's all fun. We sit and laugh about it."

Meanwhile, while all this was going on, they were nobodies in their own country. "It was weird, because we'd play shows to, like, 10,000 fans in Europe, then we'd come back home and walk down the street and no one would recognize us," Nick told the *Los Angeles Times*. "It was a humbling experience, because now we want to show everybody 'Look, this is what we've been doing.'"

The world tour experience was very important, however, because it helped establish traditions the guys still practice today—especially the preshow prayer and hug. "It's like saying, 'Let's not take any of this for granted. We're blessed.'" A.J. said in *USA Weekend* in January 1999.

So have the Backstreet Boys kept up their momentum in Europe? You bet! *Backstreet Boys* sold millions of copies worldwide and it had gone gold or platinum in more than twenty countries—even though in their own country, in 1995 and 1996, no one except their families and friends had ever heard of the Backstreet Boys.

Brian and Nick can find fast food anywhere! Here in Amsterdam they sample pommes frites—french fries—while relaxing before a show.

Their second European release, *Backstreet's Back*, debuted at number one in six European countries, shipping some 1.2 million copies across the continent, according to Jive VP of Europe Bert Meyer. And the Backstreet magic went farther than Europe. The guys were all the rage in Southeast Asia, and also in Canada. It was their popularity up in Canada that finally earned them the recognition they yearned for down in the United States, however.

By the middle of 1997, the guys were starting to feel confident enough to go back home and try out their brand of magic in their own country. "I think the [U.S.] market is ready for a group like us now," Howie said in *USA Today* in April 1997. "I think that at the time we released our first record, alternative, grunge, and urban were hot. Now we feel that pop music is starting to come back a little." He was right.

Above: Most of the guys play a musical instrument and do some of their own writing. Here, Howie strums out a tune to relax before going onstage during a UK tour.

Left: Brian reviews some publicity material while listening to tunes on the tour bus.

The Backstreet Boys, the Beatles, and the Teenage Girl

In 1964, America was invaded. Not by foreign troops. Not by aliens. But by four mop-topped Brits who had caused a real stir with American teenagers even before their airplane touched down in the States. It was much the same for the Backstreet Boys more than thirty years later when European teenagers came in droves to welcome the Yanks.

Regardless of generation, or nation, there's just something about a guy group that gets hearts racing and tongues wagging. So when your mother or father pokes fun at you about being in love with Brian or Nick or A.J. or Howie or Kevin, you just remind them about John and Paul and George and Ringo! Or if they were teenagers in the 1970s, try out David or Shaun Cassidy—or the Bee Gees for that matter. Or, if it happens to be your grandmother having a little fun with you, the words "Frank Sinatra" might be a couple you'll want to throw at her. Trust me, they'll stop—and, better still, they might take a more serious interest in the Backstreet Boys!

The Backstreet Boys perform at Radio City Music Hall in New York City, July 1998.

The Boys were accepting music awards in Europe long before American fans ever heard of them.

Chapter Five
A.J. McLean

"I'm a big ham and I gotta be out there and doing crazy stuff for no apparent reason, especially on stage."

—A.J., the Backstreet Boys Web Site

"The Crazy One": A.J.'s Vital Stats

Full name: **Alexander James McLean**

Millennium element: **Sun**

Birth date: **January 20, 1978**

Star sign: **Capricorn**

Hair: **Brown (naturally, but it changes often!)**

Eyes: **Brown**

Height: **5'9"**

Parents' names: **Denise and Robert McLean (divorced)**

Brothers and sisters: **A.J.'s an only child**

Pets: **Panda and Bear (both black-and-white shi tzus)**

Nicknames: **A.J., Bones**

Hobby: **Swimming**

Special trait: **A.J. had ten tattoos at last count—and each has a special meaning.**

Special skill: **With three series under his belt, A.J. has been on TV more than the other guys.**

Perfect mate: **She has to be into romance . . . and if she's No Doubt lead singer Gwen Stefani well, you can't get more perfect than that for A.J.!**

Right: A.J. signs videos and CDs for fans after a New York performance. Love that hat, man!

Opposite: On stage, A.J. eats up all the attention he gets from fans.

A.J.'s never too busy to stop and pose for a photo with his fans.

The nuttiest Backstreet Boy is definitely A.J. Whether he's adding another tattoo to his already picturesque bodyscape or changing the color of his hair, A.J. loves to stand out. He enjoys the attention he gets from fans—well, most of the time, that is. He told *USA Weekend* that the worst part of being a Backstreet Boy is "when you're walking in the mall and they recognize you and scream. Then everyone comes and your whole shopping day is ruined." But he doesn't mind it that much—after all, he doesn't really like to go unnoticed, either.

A.J. does loves the wild party life. When the guys are on tour, you can often find A.J. pressing clubbing buddies Kevin and Howie to hit all the hot spots with him. And A.J. is always looking for a new activity. Lately, he would really like to try out Swing dancing. As he mentioned in *Teen Beat*, "I really like Swing . . . I would love to take lessons . . . It looks like so much fun. I could wear suspenders." He's actually a big fan of the era, and counts among his idols Sammy Davis, Jr., and Frank Sinatra, who, he told *USA Weekend*, "did everything right."

Although Howie is definitely A.J.'s best friend (remember, aside from Brian and Kevin, who are cousins, Howie and A.J. have known each other the longest!), he loves all the guys like family. "The five of us are like brothers and family," he has said on

Performing in London.

numerous occasions. "I don't think you'll ever see four Backstreet Boys or two Backstreet Boys. It will always be the five of us."

A.J. was born Alexander James McLean in Palm Beach, Florida. His childhood was not as idyllic as the other guys', however. When A.J. was four, his parents spilt up, leaving his mother, Denise, to raise her young son single-handedly when his father just about disappeared from his life. That is, until just recently, when his father contacted him. They talked for a while, but A.J. is definitely proceeding with caution. "If he would do things in moderation, maybe we could get a father-son relationship back. But being so damn pushy, I just don't want to do it," A.J. told *Rolling Stone*. "He calls me every day. He drives me nuts. I don't really answer his phone calls." Certainly all of A.J.'s fans are hoping for the best and that he can work out his problems with his dad.

Another obstacle that threatened to stand in A.J.'s way is that, as a child, he had a speech impediment—not the best starting block for an aspiring actor. But A.J. has always been extremely driven, which many people might not see behind his flamboyant facade. "I always pushed myself," he told *Rolling Stone*. "To this day I take my crap seriously. If, God forbid, something happened to me where I couldn't perform, I would rather die, basically." A.J. got over his speech problem and took to the stage. His first role was as Dopey in a production of *Snow White and the Seven Dwarfs*, in which he didn't have any lines but performed physical antics that kept the audience in stitches. This led to a span of twenty-seven plays between the ages of ten and twelve!

When he was twelve, A.J. moved to Orlando with his mother to pursue his acting career. This worked out great for him as he was able to find lots of work. He sang, danced, and acted his way through high school, landing roles in three Nickelodeon TV shows: *Hi Honey, I'm Home*, *Welcome Freshman*, and *Fifteen*. He auditioned for a role in *The Mickey Mouse Club* but didn't make it in, which was fine for him because this was about the same time that he hooked up with Howie and Nick and began performing with them. A.J. felt there were greener pastures to visit—and he was absolutely right!

"Our shows are for the whole family," A.J. explained to *USA Weekend*, "younger sisters, older sisters, the cats, the dogs. We even had a dog chasing our bus. I said to Nick, 'Look, now we have animal fans! That's when you know you've made it.'"

Howie, A.J.'s mom Denise, A.J., and Kevin at *The Phantom Menace* premiere. A.J.'s mom has been a big part of A.J.'s life both at home and on the road. She used to travel with the band before A.J. turned twenty-one, and now she works as their publicist.

BACKSTREET QUIZ How well do you know . . . A.J.?

1) A.J.'s favorite European city is:
a. Berlin
b. Venice
c. Paris
d. Rome

2). You'll know A.J.'s in the room when you get a whiff of his favorite cologne, which is:
a. Obsession for Men
b. Joop
c. CK 1
d. Lagerfeld

3) A.J.'s favorite movie is:
a. *Pulp Fiction*
b. *Raiders of the Lost Ark*
c. *Goodfellas*
d. *Annie Hall*

4) What's A.J.'s favorite color?
a. Tangerine
b. Hot pink
c. Yellow
d. Lime green

5) A.J. never misses a movie starring his favorite actor:
a. Tom Cruise
b. Dustin Hoffman
c. Sean Connery
d. Mike Myers

Answers: 1: c; 2: b; 3: a; 4: c; 5: b

Who else could pull off facial hair trimmed to match his tattoos?

Chapter Six
Howie Dorough

"Acting and singing are like one for me. . . . I tried to keep them both equal so whichever one took off first was the one I was going to go with."

—Howie, in *Backstreet Boys Confidential: The Unofficial Book*

"The Sweet One": Howie's Vital Stats

Full name: **Howard Dwayne Dorough**
Millennium element: **Fire**
Birth date: **August 22, 1973**
Star sign: **Leo**
Hair: **Black**
Eyes: **Brown**
Height: **5'6"**
Parents' names: **Hoke and Paula Dorough**
Sisters and brother: **Angela, Caroline, Polly Anna, and Johnny (all at least ten years older than Howie!)**
Pets: **Missy (a cat)**
Nicknames: **Sweet D, Howie D, The Mediator**
Hobby: **Water skiing**
Special trait: **A gift for gab; Howie can talk to anyone anywhere. And when the guys argue, he's usually the one to help them see the other one's side—which is why they call him "The Mediator."**
Special skill: **When he was growing up, Howie took ballet lessons.**
Perfect mate: **She has to be a good dancer, a good conversationalist, and a hopeless romantic.**

Howie with a message for fans: Peace!

Howie croons for his
fans—they're dying just to
touch his hand!

Ever since Howie was three years old, singing "Baby Face" at
the top of his lungs standing on his grandmother's bed, his
older sister Polly Anna had been encouraging him to go into
show business. In fact, Howie's first stage role was in a production
of *The Wizard of Oz*, to which his sister had dragged him along for
an audition. Polly Anna was cast as Glenda, the good witch; Howie
made his stage debut as a munchkin!

Half Irish, half Puerto Rican, Howie was born in Orlando,
Florida, the late-born last child of Hoke and Paula Dorough.
Needless to say, with ten years between Howie and the second
youngest, Johnny, Howie grew up the family's darling—but he was
by no means spoiled. Howie's father retired from the police force
when Howie was twelve and became Howie's main caregiver.
Howie grew up with a sense of self-discipline that has served him
very well throughout his career.

Howie had made the most significant career leaps at the time he met up with A.J. and Nick. In addition to singing in the church choir as a child and performing in all sorts of school productions, Howie had already been in two films: *Parenthood* and *A Cop and a Half*—not to mention countless Disney commercials. Like A.J., he also tried out for *The Mickey Mouse Club* and didn't make it. He also auditioned for Menudo at one point, but no dice. When he got together with A.J. and Nick, though, he knew they were on to something special.

Howie is a firm believer in the kind of music the Backstreet Boys make—despite the fact that his male peers don't always see the value in what they're doing. He remembered, in *Rolling Stone*, that during their first tour—before the single, even before they had signed a recording label—"The guys would heckle us. We'd say 'You think you can do better, come on up here.' We'd sing *a cappella* and we'd have them sing along with us. When it was their turn, we'd just drop out, let them sing by themselves. It embarrassed the heck out of them." This sounds so typical of Howie, who can

Above: Howie at the 1997 Billboard Music Awards.

Opposite: Howie struts his stuff at a celebrity basketball game in Miami in January 1999.

Howie and buddy A.J. in a
brotherly embrace.

get through to anyone, no matter what situation the guys have
ever found themselves in.

Howie can talk to anyone about anything at anytime—and
make it make sense. In fact, he's often called in to settle fights
between the guys and find some kind of peaceful resolution. And
it usually works. He's the same way with his fans. Out of all the
Boys, Howie always knows the right thing to say to any fan he
meets. That's why his fans sometimes call him "Sweet D."

Out of all the guys, Howie is the most concentrated on the
future. He wants to enjoy a long career with the Backstreet
Boys—as well as a luxurious present!—but he's a show business
veteran who knows all this could be over when he wakes up in

the morning. He's the proverbial squirrel preparing for winter. Howie has used his earnings to invest in condos, and, in addition to being a Backstreet Boy, he has gotten himself involved in real estate full time—which is why the guys all tease him and call him "the businessman." But he remains practical. "We've had some tough times," he told *Teen People*. "We want to thank the fans who've not believed the hype. It's made us stronger."

In addition to concentrating on his singing, Howie is starting to get more involved with the music, writing songs and playing instruments. "We just kind of dabble with [musical instruments]," he explains. "We're not trying to proclaim to be musicians, you know, professional musicians or anything. We're not trying to be the Hansons or anything." But he's serious about it. "I just got my home studio installed, and Nick just got his installed, too. So whenever we come home, now, all the ideas we have we can put them down and get them on tape and send them to the record company. And that's a lot of fun."

Nice hat, Howie!

BACKSTREET QUIZ How well do you know . . . Howie?

1) What was Howie's best subject in school?
a. History
b. English
c. Math
d. Biology

2) What's Howie's favorite kind of food?
a. Chinese
b. Cuban
c. French
d. German

3) Howie's favorite actor is:
a. Denzel Washington
b. Harrison Ford
c. Adam Sandler
d. Tom Hanks

4) Howie's favorite beverage is:
a. Coke
b. Sprite
c. Snapple
d. Milk

5) What was Howie's stage name for the BSB audition?
a. Mike Philips
b. Tony Donetti
c. Richard Smits
d. Jack Sprat

Answers: 1: c; 2: a; 3: d; 4: b; 5: b

Chapter Seven
American Invasion

"People think we're from London or someplace. But now it's time to come home. It's important for us to be recognized here."

—Brian, in *Entertainment Weekly*, August 1997

Backstreet Boys backstage—all decked out at the Grammy Awards.

BSB versus NKOTB: Why BSB are here to stay

Part of the unfortunate backlash that the Backstreet Boys have received is that "they're just another New Kids on the Block," which is very upsetting for true Backstreet Boys fans because it just isn't so.

There are many reasons that they get burdened with this comparison, and they're all very aware of it. "We get that just because of our look and our age and everything," Nick told *USA Today*. "But comparing our style to theirs, we have a lot more R&B influences there."

Aside from their age, they also get knocked because they had the same management as the New Kids, namely Donna and Johnny Wright. But even the Wrights, as well as the big executives at the record compa-

ny, know how special the Backstreet Boys are. "The difference is that these boys can really sing, and that's a major part of our marketing strategy," Jive Records VP of A&R David McPherson has said. "We're trying to get the media to look at them differently than the New Kids and present opportunities for them to sing in public, so people can see how talented they really are."

The guys perform during an in-store appearance at the Virgin Mega Store in Times Square.

In the summer of 1997, after hitting the top of the Canadian charts, the Backstreet Boys' single "Quit Playing Games (With My Heart)," made its way to the ears of American audiences. After eating up the tunes of home-grown Hanson and the British-imported Spice Girls, Americans were eager to embrace the band that had caused such a stir overseas. Little did American listeners know that these guys had been available more than two years before, and right in their own backyard!

"Even though this is home for us, it's still a new territory, and you don't know what the reaction will be," A.J. told *USA Today* right before the single was released in the United States in April 1997. They must have been more than pleasantly surprised when "Quit Playing Games" soared to the number-four position on the charts. And the success didn't end there. When the next single, "As Long As You Love Me," jumped to number four, the guys knew it was their time to shine. The Backstreet Boys had finally made it at home.

The debut album, *Backstreet Boys*, which featured five singles that had already become huge hits overseas, was starting to set new records in the States. Suddenly Howie, A.J., Brian, Nick, and Kevin were household names all across America. And just like in Europe, the fans went crazy over the guys. From camping out at the guys' parents' houses to taking mail from their mailboxes, the fans could not get enough. Although their following was still mainly teenage girls, the Boys' longtime bodyguard reported to *Rolling Stone* that the reluctant dads and boyfriends in the audience "try to act tough, but we see them bob their heads."

The Backstreet Boys were suddenly everywhere: on *Saturday Night Live*, *The Rosie O'Donnell Show*, *Regis and Kathy Lee*—they even made an appearance on Melissa Joan Hart's Friday night sitcom, *Sabrina the Teenage Witch*.

But it wasn't all wine and roses. The next two years would prove to be times of great upheaval for them professionally—and personally. The guys (sans Nick) were forced to file a lawsuit against Pearlman and the Wrights for holding back from them millions of dollars in earnings. According to *Rolling Stone*, the guys only received $300,000 (that's total, not for each member) for all the revenues collected from the *Backstreet Boys* album, which sold more than twenty-seven million copies worldwide, plus all the promotions, tours, sales of singles—the whole kit and kaboodle. So you take $300,000, divide that by five ($60,000), then divide that by six years ($10,000) . . . suffice to say that for all that work in all that time, they were not millionaires—not by a long shot.

The guys claim that it had nothing to do with greed on their part ($10,000 for the year at forty hours a week is not even minimum wage, and the boys were working much longer hours than that!) and that they harbor no hard feelings for Pearlman and the Wrights. It was about more than money. The guys wanted to have more control over their merchandising rights—they didn't want it to get too out of hand. "David Cassidy said he had no control of merchandising," Kevin said in *USA Today*. "We're trying to control our destiny. Enough with [Backstreet] pajamas, bedsheets, lunch boxes. It was out of hand, but now we've gained control legally."

On the personal front, there was Brian's open-heart surgery; Kevin and Brian lost their grandfathers; Howie lost a sister to Lupus; and all the guys lost a great friend in Denniz Pop, the partner of Max Martin, the song master of their new album, *Millennium* (which was dedicated to Denniz). The guys just had to take some time off to regroup, which led to rumors of a breakup—until the news came out that the Backstreet Boys would soon be releasing a new album . . .

Finally, BSB reaches American fans, snagging the MTV Music Awards statue for Best Group Video in 1998.

BACKSTREET QUIZ How well do you know . . . **The Songs?**

1) Finish this line: "I'll never break your heart, I'll never make you cry . . ."

2) Who sings the lead on "I Need You Tonight?"
a. Brian
b. A.J.
c. Nick
d. Kevin

3) Which Boy helped pen "Larger Than Life"?
a. Kevin
b. Brian
c. Howie
d. A.J.

4) Which famous songwriter was recruited to help out on *Millennium*?
a. Burt Bacharach
b. Baby Face
c. Billy Joel
d. Max Martin

5) Finish this line: "Well, I should have known that I would be . . ."

Kevin Richardson

"Kevin is still Kevin. He's the same guy, he really hasn't changed that much."

—Nick on fellow
Backstreet Boy Kevin

"The Serious One": Kevin's Vital Stats

Full name: **Kevin Scott Richardson**
Millennium element: **Steel**
Birth date: **October 3, 1972**
Star sign: **Libra**
Hair: **Black**
Eyes: **Green**
Height: **6'1"**
Parents' names: **Ann and the late Jerald Richardson**
Brothers: **Jerald Jr. and Tim**
Pets: **Quincy (a black cat)**
Nicknames: **Kev, Kevvy Kev, The Train**
Hobby: **Basketball**
Special trait: **Kevin is the most determined of the group—once he gets his mind set on something, he doesn't give up—which is why his Backstreet pals call him "The Train."**
Special skill: **Kevin was a ballroom-dance instructor in Lexington, Kentucky, when he decided to branch out and move to Orlando.**
Perfect mate: **She has to have brains, personality, confidence, and class—and she has to want kids as much as he does!**

Kevin and Howie are the two oldest members of the group, and also the only two who like to sample the foods of countries they visit; the others make a beeline for McDonalds!

K evin Richardson grew up the youngest of three brothers in Lexington, Kentucky. Ironically, in the Backstreet Boys, he gets to be the big brother. "I never had a little brother," he told *USA Today*, "but now I've got four." Still, Kevin had a wonderful childhood, a perfect backdrop for his role as child music prodigy.

Kevin comes from a long line of musicians. "My grandfather was in a barbershop quartet, and everyone in my family plays music by ear," he admitted in the *Los Angeles Times*. And Kevin's mother (Brian's father's sister) sings in her church, which, like Brian, is how Kevin got his start singing in public. So as musicians themselves, Kevin's family saw a lot of talent in the young Kevin, and always pushed him toward a career in performance. Kevin's father, Jerald, especially encouraged his son to follow his dreams.

Unlike his Backstreet brothers, Kevin didn't do a lot of performing in his younger years—there isn't a long list of auditions for TV shows and other stuff on his resumé. But he did do a couple of high school productions, such as *Bye Bye Birdie* and *Barefoot in the Park*. Although he'd been playing piano since he was nine, it was the experiences on the stage that really helped make up his mind to become a performer. Still, he stuck around Lexington after high school trying to find his way; he even worked as a ballroom dance instructor for a while.

Kevin finally decided to take off to follow his dreams. With his family's support and encouragement, he wound up in Orlando, Florida. Kevin worked at Disney World and pulled the occasional deejay stint at clubs for a bit, but then tragedy entered his life. Kevin's father, his main source of encouragement and his hero, was diagnosed with cancer. Kevin shelved his dreams of stardom to see his family through the illness and his father's inevitable death.

While Kevin stuck around for a while to help his family pick up the pieces, his mom made sure he didn't get off track and pushed him to return to Orlando, which he ultimately did. Kevin stepped into the role of Aladdin at Disney World, which is what he was doing when he read the ad for a singing group on that fateful day. Kevin has not forgotten how hard his father's death has been on his mother, and although he hated being so far away from her while he was on tour in Europe, both mother and son knew it was for the best. His rise to fame has not only fulfilled his dreams but proved a blessing for his family—the devoted son just recently paid off his mother's mortgage.

"I definitely have newfound respect for the artists like Michael [Jackson] and Prince and all those other artists that not only have been successful but have been on top for a long, long time," Kevin told *USA Today*. "It's so much harder than any of us had expected." As much as he enjoys fame, however, the serious, sensitive guy, who his bandmates named "The Train" because of his relentless determination, is saddened that he doesn't always know who he can trust—his family and Backstreet brothers aside, of course. "There's a definite fear deep down in all of us of why someone's talking to you," he explained to *Teen People*. "Is it because you're Kevin or Brian, or is it because you're in a group called the Backstreet Boys? And not just in dating, but in friendships and business, too."

Surprisingly, Kevin is the only one of the Boys who's ever been engaged. It was a long time ago, and it didn't work out, but someday he'd like to be married and be a dad. But right now settling down is not in the cards. He even hesitates dating anyone because he fears that if he finds someone really special, he'll have to be away from her, and that's not how he wants it to be.

Above: Kevin was a fashion plate at the VH1 Fashion Awards.

Opposite: All the guys made it for the *Phantom Menace* premiere and party in New York City.

Kevin is usually responsible for keeping the group grounded, like a good older brother should be. The rest of the guys love him dearly, but they also respect his decisions and usually don't cross him. In the beginning, there was a little trouble between Nick and Kevin, because Kevin was so much older and Nick was such a practical joker—but all that's been resolved now. Kevin's taught Nick to be more serious; and Nick's taught Kevin to enjoy a good joke!

"I wish people would realize that we have the goods and that we're legit," Kevin told *Rolling Stone*. "We're talented, and we're not some flash in the pan. We've been together for six years." And if Kevin has anything to say about it, the guys will continue their success, earning the respect in the industry that they truly deserve.

Opposite: Kevin enjoys one of the perks of superstardom as an honorary ball boy at Arthur Ashe Stadium.

Right: Kevin holds the roses given to him by adoring fans at a party held at the Hammerstein Ballroom before a New York concert.

BACKSTREET QUIZ How well do you know . . . Kevin?

1) Kevin's favorite color is:
a. Sea green
b. Eggplant purple
c. Royal blue
d. Coral

2) If you made dinner for Kevin, he'd really like:
a. Tacos
b. Sushi
c. Burgers and fries
d. Spaghetti

3) Kevin's favorite actress is:
a. Sandra Bullock
b. Michelle Pfeiffer
c. Laura San Giacomo
d. Jennifer Love Hewitt

4) What's Kevin's favorite flick?
a. *The Spy Who Shagged Me*
b. *The Untouchables*
c. *Top Gun*
d. *Better off Dead*

5) For the first years of his life, Kevin and his family lived in a:
a. Trailer
b. Mansion
c. Log cabin
d. Apartment building

Opposite: Kevin and Nick get chummy with Sean "Puffy" Combs.

Above: Gorgeous Kevin got to walk down the runway at the VH-1 Fashion Awards, where this luscious shot was snapped.

Answers: 1: c; 2: a; 3: b; 4: c; 5: c

Chapter Nine
Millennium . . . **and Beyond**

"If we each had a song, written by each of us with our individual tastes, it would be the most outrageous album. Everything from rock, to gospel ballads, to hip-hop—it would be insane."

—A.J., in *Teen Beat*, August 1999

Showing off their various tastes in fashion, the Boys stop
for paparazzi during their 1997 tour of London.

Backstreet Boys went ten times platinum and was nominated for a Grammy. How were the guys ever going to top that? "We had so much success with the first album, [it] set us apart from everyone else," Brian told *Teen People*. But would that success carry the second one? Well, record store owners around the country were convinced that the next album, *Millennium*, would not only top *Backstreet Boys* but would set some records of its own!

Around the country, record stores expected a landslide of buyers when *Millennium* became available on May 18, 1999. They even speculated that *Millennium* would break all records for sales on its release. They were right. *Millennium* sold about 500,000 copies on its first day out—and that's not all. It also broke the record for debut-week sales set by Garth Brooks the previous year.

So what's the secret of *Millennium*'s success? "The Backstreet Boys delivered a great album, with great songs, and have worked hard over the last several years to be in this position," was Jive Senior VP/GM of sales and marketing Tom Carrabba's answer to *Billboard* magazine.

That's not all. This time, members of the group really

made their voices heard by cowriting some of the songs. Brian cowrote "Larger Than Life," which he explains is a song about the way their fans make the guys feel. "The song is all about the fans," Brian explained to *Teen Beat.* "It talks about how they affect our lives and our reality . . . when you're onstage . . . you see all these people singing your songs. It makes you feel, larger than life." Brian also lent his writing talents to the ballad "The Perfect Fan," which, he explains, is "a song about my mom . . . everyone can relate to someone who pushes you in the right direction and is there to watch over you, and help you take those steps towards the good life."

"Back to Your Heart" was cowritten by Kevin, and if you ask him if it's personal, he might confess that he may have had a special lady in mind when he wrote it. Most of the other songs were written by Max Martin, most poignantly "Show Me the Meaning of Being Lonely," which the guys see as a tribute to Denniz Pop. Martin, the Swedish song spinner who has composed tunes for such huge acts as Britney Spears and Ace of Base, was convinced that this album was his best work yet. "I've never been

The guys indulge in an upbeat number during their most recent U.S. tour.

so happy with an album," he beamed in *Teen People*. "The last album was huge, so all the [new] songs had to be hits basically, and that's not easy," he continued. "The pressure is there; you just can't touch it. You can't really talk about it, because that will make them [more] nervous."

Things were not initially that smooth with the new album, however, especially when they proposed the name. Nick recalled that "we got a lot of flack from record company reps for naming it *Millennium* because they were like, 'Oh that's so corny.' We like the name. . . . I was actually afraid someone else would use [it]." Brian is totally confident that the right name was chosen. "Bring in the *Millennium*. Bring in the Backstreet Boys," he told *Teen People*. "How else would you want to bring it in but with a slamming record."

One of the best things that happened to the guys is that they picked up a great sponsor for the *Millennium* Tour: Sears. Look for the guys in print and TV ads for the famous store. Now the Backstreet Boys will be able to do the kind of show they've always dreamed of doing, a show worthy of their exquisite talents. Not that their other shows have been mediocre. Not even close. The performances are always an explosion of sound and light and energy and costume and dance. It will be absolutely exciting to see what the new show will be like, however. The rumor is that the show will be directed by rock legend Mark Ravitz, the man behind David Bowie's groundbreaking *Ziggy Stardust* tour. The Millennium Tour kicks off in the States in Miami on September 19, 1999. They plan to perform for three months—and then hurry back home to record a Backstreet Boys Christmas album.

Otherwise, the guys have no huge future plans. Following the tour, they will perhaps start work on their next album, which they are determined will feature at least one song written by each Boy. Also, each Boy wants to get more involved in playing some of the instruments on the album. There were plans for a comic book, illustrated by the group's resident artist, Nick Carter, but it looks like this is moving to the back burner for now. "It's a dark Batman-like story, a sci-fi type of thing, and all the Backstreet Boys are characters. I believe it will open us up to male fans," Nick gushed to *USA Weekend* in January 1999. It will be about "each of us developing a power, like mutants, and battling a group of aliens who are trying to take over the world through music." That will definitely be something to keep an eye out for!

A.J., Nick, Kevin, Brian, and Howie in London, just before they were to return to their homeland.

What Are the Guys' Most Embarrassing Moments?

Hey, Backstreet Boy or not, everyone has made his or her share of goof-ups in life. Here are some of the funniest of the guys' embarrassing moments (and believe me—there are lots more where these came from!).

NICK: During a concert, Nick accidentally "pushed" Howie right off the stage and into the audience!

BRIAN: Kicked a shoe off during a dance number. The shoe flew across the stage, and Brian had to keep dancing in his sock until he could make his way over to where the shoe landed!

A.J.: Started a fire during a show in Germany when he accidentally tossed one of his shirts over a light during a costume change!

KEVIN: Slipped on a pack of cigarettes some fan in Europe had thrown up on the stage during a performance as a gift. See how dangerous cigarettes are!

HOWIE: Howie once had to sing his solo completely *a cappella* when the whole sound system went out right in the middle of one of his songs!

The boys say that they are all as close as brothers, and that like brothers, they don't always get along—but they manage to work through their differences and stay together.

The guys look demure before the 1997 MTV Europe Awards. A year later they would be honored by MTV in the United States.

Bibliography

"Babe Poll Results: The Celebs You Begged For!"
Teen magazine (September 1998): 84.

"Backstreet Boys Believe: 'You Have to Follow Your
Heart.'" Teen Beat (August 1999): 70

"Backstreet Boys: Get Ready for the New Millennium."
Teen Beat (June 1999): 7.

"Backstreet Boys: Interview of the Month." Teen Beat
(August 1997): 20–21.

"Backstreet's Back with Millennium." SuperTeen
(August 1999): 26.

Boucher, Geoff. "The Making of Heartthrobs Inc."
Los Angeles Times (January 24, 1999): 4.

Brooks, Amy and Jeremy Helligar. "Where the Boys Are."
People Weekly (September 14, 1998): 238.

Brunner, Rob. "Boys Power." Entertainment Weekly
(June 4, 1999): 9.

Carter, Jane. The Heart and Soul of Nick Carter.
New York: Penguin Putnam, 1998.

Christman, Ed. "Backstreet Could Hit 1 Mil. In 1st Week."
Billboard (May 29, 1999): 3.

Cotter, Kelly-Jane. "Backstreet Boys Are the New
Heartthrob Act on the Block." Gannett News Service
(October 9, 1998)

de Ste. Croix, Philip (editor). Backstreet Boys:
The Unofficial Book. New York: Billboard Books,
1998.Dunn, Jancee. "The Backstreet Boys' Year in Hell."
Rolling Stone (May 27, 1999): 42–47.

Farber, Jim. "Where the Boys Are." Entertainment Weekly
(May 21, 1999): 73.

Finkelstein, Alex. "Backstreet Boy's Firm Sues N.Y. Record
Company." Orlando Business Journal (September 18,
1998): 3.

———. "Backstreet Boys: Local Manager Milked Millions."
Orlando Business Journal (September 11, 1998): 1.

Jaeger, Lauren. "'Everybody' Packing In for Backstreet
Boys." Amusement Business (July 20, 1998): 1.

Jones, Steve. "Bringing Fame Home: Florida Quintet is
Playing 'Games' for Keeps Now." USA Today (April 1,
1997): 1D.

Karger, Dave. "Flashes." Entertainment Weekly (October
30, 1998): 16.

———. "So Shoot Me!" Entertainment Weekly (September
4, 1998): 24.

LeBlanc, Larry. "Backstreet Boys Riding a Wave: Canadian
Success Began in Quebec." Billboard (December 13,
1997): 52.

"Lunch With Nick and the Backstreet Boys." SuperTeen
(August 1999): 20–25

Majewski, Lori. "The Boys Are Back." Teen People
(June/July 1999): 100–04.

Mayfield, Geoff. "Bigger Still." Billboard (May 29, 1999):
100.

Nichols, Angie. Backstreet Boys Confidential: The
Unofficial Book. London: Virgin Books, 1998.

Ross, Mike. "Boys Will Be Boys." The Edmonton Sun
(May 15, 1999): 44.

Sexton, Paul. "Backstreet Boys Become Global Priority
for Jive." Billboard (November 1, 1997): 9.

Sinclair, Tom. "The Orlando Magic Backstreet Boys:
Florida's Prefab Sprouts Take Root." Entertainment
Weekly (August 15, 1997): 72.

"The Twenty-one Hottest Stars Under Twenty-one."
Teen People (June/July 1999): 56.

"25 Most Intriguing People of the Year." People Weekly
(December 28, 1998): 114.

Weingarten, Marc. "And They Can Sing, Too." Los Angeles
Times (January 4, 1998).

Zaslow, Jeffrey. "Backstage With the Backstreet Boys."
USA Weekend (January 10, 1999): 14.

Web Sites

Official International Backstreet Boys Website:
www.backstreetboys.com

Alison's Backstreet Boys Wonderland:
www.geocities.com/SunsetStrip/Backstage/1823

Andrea's Unofficial Backstreet Boys Internet Fan Club:
www.geocities.com/SouthBeach/Lagoon/7620/FrameSet1.html

Anywhere For You:
www.geocities.com/SunsetStrip/Studio/9847/

Backstreet Boys Connection:
www.geocities.com/SunsetStrip/Lounge/3367/

BSB Direct: Backstreet Boys Directory:
surf.to/backstreet.boys/

Jill's Backstreet Boys Heaven:
www.execulink.com/~wmgp/Default.htm

Singapore Backstreet Boys Homepage:
www.ashweb.com/bsb/

T-one's Backstreet Bar:
www.geocities.com/SouthBeach/Surf/4167/

Backstreet Boys Planet:
www.geocities.com/SunsetStrip/Palms/2109/

Backstreet Boys Celebrity Site:
www.bestcelebritysites.com/backstreet-boys

Canadian Backstreet Boys Webring:
www.myna.com/~sacart/ring.htm

Frick and Frack's Backstreet Boys Heaven:
members.tripod.com/~Frick_and_Frack/main.html

Hong Kong Backstreet Boys:
www.geocities.com/SunsetStrip/Lounge/2397/

Yoni's BSB Fantasy:
www.geocities.com/Hollywood/Set/6331

Photography Credits

Index